Other books by Peggy Salvatore:

30 Days of WhizDom

Working with SMEs: A Guide to Gathering and
Organizing Content from Subject Matter Experts

Finding Your SMEs: Capturing Knowledge from Retiring Subject
Matter Experts in Your Organization Before They Leave

Working in SMEville: A Workbook

Retaining Expert Knowledge: What to Keep
in an Age of Information Overload

30 DAYS TO SUCCESS IN THE NEW ECONOMY

YOUR ROLE IN HISTORY AS AN ENTREPRENEUR
WITH A NEW COVID-19 AFTERWORD

PEGGY SALVATORE, MBA

BALBOA.PRESS
A DIVISION OF HAY HOUSE

Copyright © 2020 Peggy Salvatore, MBA.

All rights reserved. No part of this book may be used or reproduced by any means, graphic, electronic, or mechanical, including photocopying, recording, taping or by any information storage retrieval system without the written permission of the author except in the case of brief quotations embodied in critical articles and reviews.

Balboa Press books may be ordered through booksellers or by contacting:

Balboa Press
A Division of Hay House
1663 Liberty Drive
Bloomington, IN 47403
www.balboapress.com
844-682-1282

Because of the dynamic nature of the Internet, any web addresses or links contained in this book may have changed since publication and may no longer be valid. The views expressed in this work are solely those of the author and do not necessarily reflect the views of the publisher, and the publisher hereby disclaims any responsibility for them.

The author of this book does not dispense medical advice or prescribe the use of any technique as a form of treatment for physical, emotional, or medical problems without the advice of a physician, either directly or indirectly. The intent of the author is only to offer information of a general nature to help you in your quest for emotional and spiritual well-being. In the event you use any of the information in this book for yourself, which is your constitutional right, the author and the publisher assume no responsibility for your actions.

Any people depicted in stock imagery provided by Getty Images are models, and such images are being used for illustrative purposes only.
Certain stock imagery © Getty Images.

Print information available on the last page.

ISBN: 978-1-9822-5279-3 (sc)
ISBN: 978-1-9822-5280-9 (e)

Balboa Press rev. date: 08/24/2020

Dear Reader,

This edition contains minor edits and a few statistical updates from the original 2015 Kindle publication.

I can be reached at workingwithsmes@gmail.com.

Thank you for reading.

Pepy Salvatore

Contents

Day 1: Introduction to a Fantastical Journey..................1

WEEK 1: Defining the New Economy
Day 2: Internet Entrepreneurs and Frontier Mentality.......7
Day 3: Historical Business Pivot Points..........................9
Day 4: Twitter Feed from Syria....................................11
Day 5: Low Cost, High Quality and Personal Service in the New Economy..13
Day 6: The Virtues of Internet Joe................................15
Day 7: Products in the New Economy..........................18
Day 8: To Infinity and Beyond.....................................21

WEEK 2: The Seven Traits of Internet Joe
Day 9: Internet Stardom...27
Day 10: Characteristics of the New Entrepreneur..........29
Day 11: Integrity..31
Day 12: Creativity..33
Day 13: Adventurous...35
Day 14: Confidence...37
Day 15: Knowledge..39

WEEK 3: Internet Infrastructure
Day 16: Imagine Leadership and Management..............43
Day 17: Imagine Finance..45
Day 18: Imagine Marketing..49
Day 19: Imagine Sales..51
Day 20: Imagine Manufacturing...................................53
Day 21: Imagine Inventory and Delivery......................55
Day 22: Imagine Your Learning Organization...............57

WEEK 4: Your Resources

Day 23: Financing 61
Day 24: Revenue 63
Day 25: Human Capital 65
Day 26: Buildings and Machinery 67
Day 27: Communications Network 69
Day 28: Education and Training 71
Day 29: Health and Wellness 73
Day 30: Entrepreneur's Checklist 74

Afterword: A Post-COVID-19, Non-Fragile World 75

Day 1: Introduction to a Fantastical Journey

> *A new scientific proof is not usually presented in a way to convince its opponents. Rather, they die off, and a rising generation is familiarized with the truth from the start.*
>
> – Max Planck

SOME PEOPLE SAY the world economy is coming apart at the seams. I disagree.

Just like most everyone else in the last few decades, I watch the world from my computer and it is a fantastical place. The nimble entrepreneurs in the Internet economy are zigging while major corporations are zagging. Zigging is the new orange.

Is the world economy coming apart at the seams? Heck, no. The world is undergoing a major shift. Anyone stuck in the old paradigm is feeling the dislocation and the loss. Those hanging on trying to bring back large, lumbering, industrial manufacturing – or even trying to keep alive a monetary system based on physical representations of value – are going to feel like things are coming apart at the seams. They are still zagging.

Customer experience is driving this new economy. Those who are zigging are responding to their potential markets in massively impressive ways. Learning is no longer a one-way street. For example, I write this not from a perch of unimpeachable wisdom (ask anyone who knows me!). But rather, I write this book from a place of inquisitiveness that is part of a burgeoning online conversation among techies, marketers, leadership gurus and innovators of all stripe. This book is intended as part of the conversation. That is why it started as a one-month-long blog collection, thus the original title "30 Days to the New Economy".

Inspired by what I'd learned online from various Internet entrepreneurs, I posted this little book as a series of blogs and then published it as an ebook at the same time – an ebook for people who would like to have this content all in one place.

This is Your Time to Build

Internet entrepreneurs are building the New Economy by being able to respond instantaneously to real customers on the ground all around the world in real time. I've been studying them and these people are nothing short of brilliant, amazing and generous.

Due to this magnificent and spontaneous development of the New Economy, today there are more people who don't know how to run a business, running a business. Problems beget solutions instantaneously now. Help is available, lots of it, online and much of it for free. The amount of not just information but excellent education and great content is on the Internet at no cost. For the monthly price of access to an Internet service provider, anyone can learn, have, do or know just about anything or anyone.

I used to wonder, hmmmm, what is the business model here? We can access valuable content for free. The dot.com bust at the turn of the 21st Century appeared to signal that online businesses could not be monetized. In retrospect, obviously that was wrong. People figured out how to make online businesses profitable. Given motivation, inspired humans will find a way to make money doing anything. Example: I paid $5 for a pet rock in a box when I was a kid. Case closed.

Given that premise, it was only a matter of time until creative humans found a way to make massive amounts of money commensurate with the massive amounts of value to be found online.

Sources

The knowledge is this little book is not original. In fact, this content is highly derivative. I will give credit where it is due. For nine months in 2015, I studied the Internet economy and the entrepreneurs who are building it. My quest started simply. I built two blogs and wanted to fit them into a business plan. That started a journey that was nothing short of fantastic. I discovered quite quickly that there is a phenomenal amount of highly valuable free information in the form of well-done training. Superlatives abound here because they are justified. Free webinars, free ebooks, free podcasts, free every-imaginable-kind-of-thing-you-want-to-know is available, and I dedicated myself to consuming as much as possible. Online content led me to a new crop of physical books and seminars, as well. So, it isn't all virtual and it isn't all free, but the virtual environment is the glue that holds all the physical pieces together.

I dedicated many hours a day to consuming free content across many disciplines including

- Business development and entrepreneurship
- Internet business structure and technology
- Personal growth
- Leadership
- Blogging, podcasting, webinar and ebook development
- Motivational and spiritual underpinnings of business success
- And more…

I've done the research. In fact, my obsession with consuming everything I could find led me to be dubbed "Webinar Woman" by my kids who found me watching, and participating in, webinars at all times of the day and evening. Here, in small, digestible chunks, I am going to distill for you the best of the best content and information that I have found to date and relate it to your life as an entrepreneur in the new economy.

CHARGE: Your 30-Day Plan

I designed this ebook as *30 Days to Success in the New Economy* because I want you to read it one day at a time for a month. Please do me that one favor.

Here's how: Read this book one page at a time over 30 days, much as you would a daily article. Let each day's thought sink in.

Here's why: When we take in one small nugget of information and think about it, we make it ours and it becomes a part of the way we see the world. That's the way the brain works. One little piece of information at a time sinking in slowly and building upon prior knowledge. If you try to digest this whole book all in one sitting, you won't absorb the subtleties in the message and be able to live it in the same way.

In this short book, I am going to take you down a path to explain the new economy and your role in it. Think about each day's message, one day at a time. Ruminate on it and discuss it.

When you've done that, bit by bit, over the period of a month, I would appreciate if you would get back to me and let me know your role in the new economy. What's your contribution? I want to know your part in building a new, integrated, humane world…on the Internet, of course.

See you tomorrow for Day 2.

Week 1
Defining the New Economy

Day 2: Internet Entrepreneurs and Frontier Mentality

IF YOU ARE building a business online in the new economy, you are a frontier person. You have figuratively hitched your wagon to your horse and lined up with the wagon train. Imagine yourself in 19th Century America, venturing out to the new Western frontier searching for gold, circa 1840.

When I started my career 25 years ago, I took a small consulting gig at the University of Pennsylvania helping the development office build its first website. I took some html classes at he university as part of the job to write the website content. The Penn development department built the first donor recognition site in the world. In the world. The first.

As part of the job, I had to investigate whether we could get digital rights to legendary opera singer Marion Anderson's recording library. I discussed the intellectual property challenges of this endeavor with the music department of Indiana University in Bloomington, Indiana, one of the places where these questions were first considered. I talked to attorneys who were still working out how much a of a copyrighted work we could republish online before violating the owners' rights. Seriously. Lawyers were just beginning to entertain those ideas in the last years of the 20th Century.

Then sometime around the end of that assignment, we got wind of some amazing new software that allowed me to build the website without inserting the html coding. I saw Windows for the first time. Since we were rounding the last bend of that project, I never actually benefitted from the new technology but we saw the changes coming.

I bring this up to say that I've watched the development of the Internet at times as more than just a bystander. I have glimpses of where we started not that long ago. Considering where we are today from that vantage point, I believe we have only just begun to develop the new economy. However, in the last few years we hit an inflection point that is allowing the Internet to take the world economy in a new direction.

People far smarter than me are talking about this in much more sophisticated ways. My purpose here is to encourage the online entrepreneur who is a small businessperson to get in the wagon train. Getting into the Internet business space now is akin to buying gold at $390 an ounce. You think it can't go any higher, and you couldn't be more wrong!

If you are thinking about whether to offer your products and services online to a global marketplace from your own virtual storefront, consider it $390 gold.

Or taking it back one more historical notch to where we began this article, you are panning for gold from the back of your Conestoga wagon.

Day 3: Historical Business Pivot Points

YESTERDAY, I TALKED about the fact that Internet business opportunities are the new $390 an ounce gold. It's going to go way higher! I also likened the technological frontier to early Americans who joined a wagon train to head into the Western American frontier in the middle of the 19th Century looking for unmined opportunities.

In a virtual world, the unmined opportunities are virtual, too. If you think about the history of business over the last 500 years in a linear way, it is clear that we are heading into a third revitalization of the world economy as people adapt to the new opportunities that technology has opened. Some have referred to this epoch as the Third Wave.

In the first wave of business opportunity, after sailors proved to mapmakers that the world was not flat, global business opportunities opened up. A merchant class emerged and dislodged the traditional power centers built around the kings and kingdoms of antiquity. Essentially, global tradewinds democratized business. Wealth spread to a whole large new group of people willing to take risks.

The establishment of the American colonies on a large, undeveloped land mass created yet more opportunities for new political and economic models to be tested safely away from the old, established controls of entrenched power. Merchant mentality spread to the previously disenfranchised masses and the small business owner was born, Mom and Pop shops proliferated beyond the old world butcher-baker-candlestick maker model. Mom and Pops opened banks. Mom and Pops built all types of small businesses to support the growing manufacturing base built on bigger dollars funded by oil, coal, lumber, railroad and textile tycoons of the late 19th Century. A few Mom and Pops became franchises and corporations of their own.

In the 20th Century, opportunity spread down to Everyman. It spread the same way that technology and genetics spread throughout human history – mostly through war -but not more frequently aided by commerce.

Progress through commerce became the late 20th Century model. It started to appear that the world economy would advance by peaceful means. War, it seemed, was becoming an outdated method of transferring knowledge, wealth, power and genetics.

Then, in the first decade of the 21st Century, something went horribly awry. War overtook commerce as the global force for economic power. As we look at the trajectory of history, however, it doesn't look like war is a sustainable model for economic power and growth any longer. Let me suggest that war is having its last stand, albeit a very nasty one.

The unrelenting wars of today, threatening huge swaths of humanity and the land on which they live, seem more like the last gasp of a dying paradigm. The Internet, and the connectivity of Everyman, everywhere, is the New Economy.

How dare I say that? Stay tuned tomorrow.

Day 4: Twitter Feed from Syria

REMEMBER THE ARAB Spring? More recently, remember the Hong Kong protests? What was that, anyway?

People protesting for freedom, I think.

People throwing off the shackles of oppression as portrayed by the press. That was the official meme. Like King George issuing an edict to the American colonies, the official meme was received with a jaundiced eye by the people in the middle of the action and their Internet friends around the globe.

Let's face it. People are playing video games and checkers with other people all around the world, all the time. Not to mention that global business ties keep everyone in close proximity to everyone else via a short jet hop or Skype. People get to know each other. It gets harder each day for an official story to go unchallenged. So it was with the Arab Spring.

As tumult rocked the Middle East, video game friends texted each other around the globe. They started Twitter feeds. People talked about what was going on.

This dynamic affects business. At the same time as global corporations can spread influence instantaneously, so can the small online entrepreneur. If knowledge is power, power is no longer hierarchical. Power is flat. It is matrixed. It favors the nimble.

Admittedly, global corporations are masters of SEO and the Google search engine. But the Internet entrepreneur has a real shot at reaching customers in his space using any number of networking opportunities in his field by darting around, past, over and under the global giants.

The average Internet Joe can connect with other Internet Joes and Janes in small- to medium-sized businesses and make an excellent living working for individuals who need his expertise. Like the global video game friends texting real-time human concern during the Arab Spring, personal networks have a flexibility and humanity that allows them to reach people on a level that the major players cannot.

The Internet offers small service and product providers the same, if not better, opportunities for personal service and connection to many potential customers around the globe as huge multinational corporations. Customers benefit from low-cost, high-quality, personal service using Internet Joe businesses operating in the new economy.

This democratization of knowledge and power has leveled the business playing field. It has also leveled the political playing field which is, if not the same thing, something very highly related and correlated. For as politics attempts to control who gets what, and who decides, the proliferation of information puts control into the hands of the average Internet Joe. He is the customer and the provider as the flattened power matrix envelopes everyone with an Internet connection. From this vantage point, new products and services are being developed in a way that is not just close to the customer but are being developed in conjunction with the customer.

Also, because average Internet Joe is everywhere, all the time, the New Economy transcends borders, nations and politics.

Stick around for Day 4 to find out how this affects commerce.

Day 5: Low Cost, High Quality and Personal Service in the New Economy

CUSTOMERS BUYING FROM you, the Internet entrepreneur in the New Economy, enjoy high-quality, low-cost, personal service. When they buy from a major corporation, they can only get one out of three. Internet Joe has cost and customer service advantages that elude the big boys.

High Quality: The owner of a small Internet business is often a former employee or consultant with a large national corporation. That means the small Internet business is run with the same degree of expertise and quality as you get from a major player without the major price tag. When the global corporation laid off its expertise, that talent found another outlet and became Internet Joe.

Low Cost: With a virtual retail storefront, the cost of business for Internet Joe is minimal. So the pricing of products and services through an entrepreneurial Internet business is far lower than the global enterprise that is supporting a huge infrastructure. In fact, it has turned what used to be the price advantage of scale on its head. In the days of large manufacturing dominance, bigger meant competitive pricing due to volume. Today, in the New Economy, bigger means more overhead and higher fixed costs. Now, the small business entrepreneur holds the price advantage.

Personal Customer Service: When you buy a product or service form an Internet entrepreneur, he is very happy to have your business. He is running his little virtual store to meet your specific needs. You are his bread and butter, so he is responsive and agile. That means as your needs evolve and the Internet entrepreneur sees the evolution by staying in close personal contact, he can respond and change with you in lockstep.

Due to small size, Internet Joe as the virtual Mom and Pop can pivot long before large corporation get the word that the market has changed. It can take a large corporation a year or more to engage its strategic planning office, hire a consultancy, conduct an environmental scan, do a SWOT analysis, report to the board, and consider a change in direction. Meanwhile, the Internet entrepreneur is at the customer's side.

Internet entrepreneurs are usually hungry critters. Like their forefathers and foremothers, the Mom and Pops, they staked out their virtual storefront (got a url), pay rent (server space), pay vendors (Internet services to run their businesses such as mail clients, shopping cart software, writers, graphic designers, etc.) and worry about their online enterprises 24/7. They probably sweep their own virtual doorstep or hire the kid next door to do it.

That kind of responsibility is a great place for customers to send their business. These small online business owners understand their customers.

Tomorrow, let's talk more about the virtues of online business owners.

Day 6: The Virtues of Internet Joe

IT TAKES A lot of hustle to open your own business.

Recently, I was at a local meeting of SCORE (retired executives who give advice to small business owners) and met a young married couple starting a boutique brewery. Location, licenses, equipment, employees…they had a lot to consider and some real hassles. But it was worth it. They will end up making their own *beer*.

Internet entrepreneurship is the same kind of hustle. He might not be hoisting vats, but Internet Joe does some heavy lifting. Think about it. He will integrate years of expertise (could be 2, could be 50) to come up with a product or service that will provide value to people somewhere, anywhere on this planet. That's a pretty wide swath to cut, so Internet Joe is always thinking.

1. Confidence: Internet Joe has enough confidence to believe he has something to offer and is willing to put in the time, effort and money to offer it.
2. Knowledge: He has a defined skill set that he may have used, or is still using, at a corporate job, but he has acquired other skills and knowledge that he did not use in his tightly defined corporate role. He is anxious to use these skills and knowledge in his new Internet business.
3. Dependability: He opened the business for a few reasons, including but not limited to the need for an income. By taking the chance of investing both time and money in developing the Internet business, Joe has already proven that he is a go-getter and that he is responsible. Customers can depend on delivery from Internet Joe.
4. Creativity: Internet Joe has the energy and the creativity to build a business online from scratch. He also has the ability to put that kind of thinking to work for customers. And all

those skills that weren't used by the last employer? Now's the time to figure out how to integrate his interest in fine art with his sales and marketing expertise.
5. Risk-taker: Joe took a risk by putting himself and his products, services and ideas out for sale to the public. That investment of time, money and creativity to build the business came at the risk of not doing something else with those resources. It also came at the risk that his endeavor could meet with crickets.
6. Integrity: This is the core requirement for any business person online and offline. Your word is your bond. You can be trusted and you respect yourself as well as everyone you come in contact with. Without integrity, you have nothing in business. Internet Joe is putting himself in the public eye and subjecting himself to levels of scrutiny heretofore impossible without investing in private investigation services.
7. Adventurous: The Internet is new. Even if you are following a proven model in your online business, you are bound to uncover some new ways of doing things and improving upon the existing system. Because Internet business is in its infancy (yes, it still is!), Internet Joe is learning along with everyone else. Internet entrepreneurs are learning together, and there is a lot of room for innovation.

Certain personal qualities are essential for success in any business. With an industry that is new, people who succeed will be among the first to find effective ways of operating in this environment. Businesses and products have a life cycle. The business cycle is traditionally divided into four segments: early adopters, pragmatists, conservatives and skeptics. "The Chasm" is the space between the innovative early adopters and the majority of early pragmatist entrants when a majority of people jump on to a new idea. I reproduce this graph here to suggest that we are crossing the chasm now. The early adopter phase is the place where history is made and the pragmatists are where the money is made. It is where you are right now.

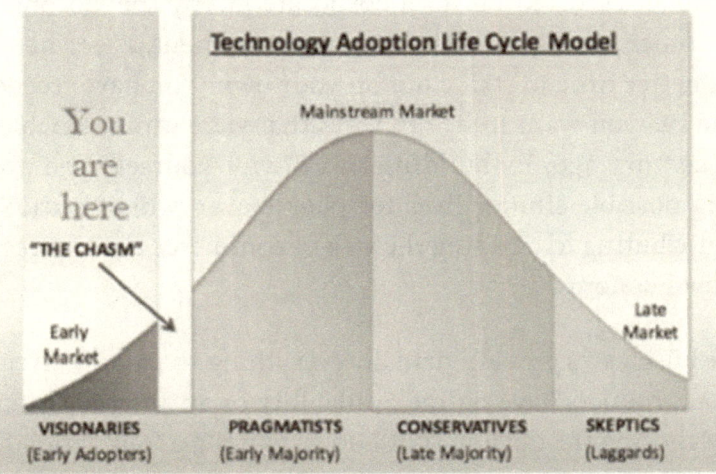

The seven traits I listed above are essential for success at this early phase in Internet business history. I will dedicate seven days talking about the success traits next week during Week 2, the Success Traits of Internet Joe.

There are a lot of Internet Joes in the New Economy. Are you one of the Frontier People staking your claim?

Day 7: Products in the New Economy

WHETHER YOU ARE a young entrepreneur, a mid-career professional escorted out of a corporate job by the Corona virus or a boomer taking the slow road to retirement, there has never been a better time to strike out on your own. You have freedom to live the life you want to live in ways that were unimaginable even a half century ago. By building this life for yourself, you are also making possible similar lives for people everywhere because you are contributing to building the web of commerce that is becoming the New Economy.

Online businesses provide virtually everything – virtually. Even most physical products have online availability or an Internet gateway. I risk belaboring the obvious, but I do so to build a foundation for the reader to appreciate both the pace of change and the promise of this accelerating opportunity. Essentially, if something can be had, it can be found, purchased and delivered using the Internet. At no time was this more obvious to everyone than during the Corona virus global lockdown when we ordered food, toiletries, medications and, heck, wine, online to be delivered safely to our door.

With this kind of limitless opportunity, it is clear that the Internet entrepreneur can carve out a niche for himself no matter his background or experience. Do you garden? Blog, write an ebook, post photos, host a webinar, offer online advice. My garden would not be so abundant were it not for Megan Cain, a woman from Madison, Wisconsin who uses her own home garden to tutor aspiring vegetable gardeners around the world with her videos, blogs and books.

Were you a marketing executive before your company was acquired and you were offered a severance package? Your skills are very valuable as you apply your expertise to the new products, services, customers and markets opening up.

Are you a mechanic specializing in vintage cars? Start a YouTube channel where you demonstrate restoration techniques, sell hard-to-find parts, host a forum and do it all behind a pay wall where car enthusiasts can buy a membership to access your exclusive content, your expertise, and all the other *afficianados* who are attracted to your business.

Spiritual gurus, leadership mentors, management experts, personal coaches and business development educators are growing a large consulting niche to aid entrepreneurs finding their way as businessowners in this environment. If you want to know how to choose a product or service to offer for sale, how to package it, where to find customers, how to appeal to them, and how to set up the mechanics of a virtual business, there is an army of experts who have developed models you can adopt.

Because the New Economy is truly a frontier right now, many of the opportunities are exactly in the kinds of products and services needed to build the model. The business model itself is not yet firmly established, When colonists set out for the Wester American frontier in the mid-19th Century, they set out from several specific points of departure where merchants had set up stores that specialized in the goods they would need for their travel. You found blacksmiths and dry goods grocers, wagon makers and tool suppliers. This particular point in time is the point of departure for the New Economy – this time it is not a physical location but a virtual one, reflecting the nature of the adventure. Rack servers, website designers and content creators are the kinds of businesses you will find at your point of departure as you venture out into the Internet frontier.

It may at times feel like we have arrived. Don't be fooled. Given the possibilities envisioned by futurists with a solid grounding in technology, physics, chemistry and biology, the actual destination of this trek is not visible from our vantage point. When you think you've arrived because you encounter a huge market, let me suggest it is the Mississippi River, not the Pacific Ocean. For non-US readers, the Mississippi River is a wide body of water that divides the United States in half. When you've reached it, while it appears impressive, you're not quite halfway across the continent.

With most opportunities still undiscovered, as you decide the products and services you can offer as an Internet entrepreneur, let your decision be guided by your imagination. Trust your instincts. Study the terrain. Steadily roll along. You will discover what lies ahead and be among the first, even when it doesn't seem that you are. And stay close to your customers because they will tell you what is up ahead.

Like guides, trust your customer requests because they will lead the way to the frontier of the New Economy.

Day 8: To Infinity and Beyond

GRASP THE FACT that we are living on the cusp of incredible opportunity. The amount of information available to us instantaneously is staggering, and we have come to take it for granted.

Let me contrast to just 20 years ago when I did health policy research. Before writing a white paper, I had to write physical letters or make a landline phone call to Washington D.C. to the U.S. Government Printing Office to request government documents. Then I would wait a week or two until some diligent librarian gathered the documents and sent me a bulky yellow envelope stuffed with the precious statistics that I sought.

Since I did a lot of government-related policy work at that time, most of my contact was with the U.S. GPO. The GPO was arguably one of the most responsive organizations I encountered. For data and studies not conducted by the U.S. government, gathering information was more challenging. Non-government-generated research required me to spend time at a local public or university library getting to know the research librarians, hunting through dusty stacks and filling out paper request forms to be sent into the library system to look for information. Imagine the limitations of linear indexes. No embedded links. No Google search engines. Books, studies and reports were listed in sets of thick, hard-backed tomes lining the research shelves of local libraries. Legal and medical research required similar effort.

That linear aspect of gathering information first required that you had a clue what you were looking for. Nobody was pushing information to your inbox because you expressed an interest in a topic. That linear aspect of research also limited the way that knowledge was built. You only knew the information that you specifically sought, so your research would have a defined trajectory from a specific point.

Today, global consulting firms like Deloitte and IBM make white papers available for download in my inbox literally every day. I can't begin to consume all the information that is interesting to me. I now know to look for knowledge that I could not have even imagined existed two decades ago. My research now has multiple starting points and can take me in an almost limitless number of directions. Knowledge indeed has become exponential. After all, anyone can edit a Wikipedia entry, all 4.5 billion of us with an Internet connection (as of Q1 2020 accessed at https://internetworldstats.com/stats.htm). In 1995, less than 1% of the world's population had an Internet connection. I was one of them, but connected to what? We really hadn't begun to explore the potential of what would reside online.

This evolutionary process repeats itself for everything.

Not too long ago, if I wanted new shoes, I walked to the shoe store, looked at a limited selection of colors, styles and sizes, and either settled for whatever was in my size or ordered something more to my liking through the retail store and waited for delivery. Some online catalogues have delivered products directly to consumers since the early 1900s, but with a few notable exceptions, catalog purchases were considered low quality and even more limited selection than the venerable old department stores.

You may think I am belaboring the obvious. You may be yawning. Imagine, though, that I describe life only 25 years ago, when today's college graduates were teething. The speed of knowledge has grown exponentially, so much that by 2015 Ray Kurzweil was suggesting that half of all data available had been collected in the previous two years. Today, IBM is suggesting that knowledge doubles every 24 hours.

What are the gems hiding in that data? How much more will we know by next year? What other assumptions and paradigms will be smashed next year, next month, next week?

Your ability to collect and process information makes you part of this surge toward a future none of us can yet fully grasp, although some futurists have come very close. Raw data has no inherent value but the interpretation of that data is priceless. Boiled down to its simplest essence, economics is the trading of value among individuals, corporations and nations. We are accruing a mind-boggling amount of value in transactions involving information, goods and services occurring in milliseconds simultaneously among billions of interconnected humans today, right now, as you are reading this.

The New Economy is just breaking out. To quote from that great Toy Story character, Buzz Lightyear, we are headed "to infinity and beyond."

Week 2
The Seven Traits of Internet Joe

Day 9: Internet Stardom

IN THE 1960S, pop art hero Andy Warhol was credited with saying that "everyone gets their 15 minutes of fame." He said that in the relatively innocent new era of radio and television. At the time, for a population most of whom grew up with their nose to the grindstone laboring at survival jobs, that seemed both outrageous and yet almost true. We all know people who've been interviewed by the media; even your sister might be approached by a reporter holding a microphone while she's walking her dog in the park. But before the Internet when Warhol made that statement, you still had to get through a few filters, no matter how thin, before grabbing your 15 minutes. Those filters might have been a newspaper reporter covering a fire, a television producer looking for contestants for a game show, or a book publisher looking for the next *Gone With The Wind*.

Contrast that to today. Internet Joe is not subject to filters. That is, no filters except his own. Under his own volition, Internet Joe can get a url with hisname.com, put up a video on YouTube and publicize it to the world on Facebook. Internet stardom is wholly within one's personal discretion. And except for $5 a month for the cost of a website, all this stardom is free.

For the average self-absorbed teenager or aspiring garage rock band, imagine the possibilities. No, better than imagine them, just surf Instagram, Facebook and YouTube to see what the unfiltered masses look like and how they behave. Then ponder for a moment the value of filters, defined as professionals with judgment, deciding what is worthy of public attention. Might educated, critical judgment have a place in this cacophony?

Just for fun, turn that last paragraph on its head. Surf Instagram, Facebook and YouTube to see what the unfiltered masses consider valuable. Then ponder for a moment the hurdle that professional filters created. By appointing themselves moderators of public taste and *morés*, corporations and governments held all the power before the Internet gained the momentum to determine the direction of humanity. People were driven into moral and cultural cattle chutes. The cows are free.

Big-time TV and movie stars were the people who made it through the process, whatever that was. Internet stars are people who choose to put themselves out as a brand. In the areas of business, entertainment and even just average-Joe-dom, people who are branding themselves and their name have had massive success making themselves Internet stars. The personal face and name as a brand exude trust that has great value in the oceans of information out there.

People who are willing to put their smiling visage on their emails and website create trust. Trust breeds business. It always has and it always will. We do business with people, not pixels. Internet stardom means success for Internet Joe.

Have you branded yourself? Do people know what you look like and do they know your story? Do they know what you think? Or do they at least *think* they know what you think? Can they hear your voice?

If the answer is yes to these questions, you are a brand.

Day 10: Characteristics of the New Entrepreneur

Nimble. Responsive. Personal.

ABOUT 10 YEARS ago, when my three kids were all in high school, I decided to go back to school to fulfill a dream to get my degree in economics. Okay, geek alert. Not every girl's dream is to study the dismal science. But it was mine.

A for-profit online college called Cardean University advertised an MBA with a specialization in economics and strategy. The curriculum had been developed by professors from The London School of Economics, the University of Chicago and Stanford. I reasoned that they couldn't advertise that fact if it weren't true. I still wasn't convinced of the value of an online degree in the real world. I phoned a friend. I asked her if an online MBA would be akin to getting your degree on the back of a matchbook cover. She said not anymore. In the real world, virtual degrees count. Eventually, Cardean was sold and my degree is from a bricks-and-mortar school. And I learned real stuff that I still use. I had classmates all around the globe, many from corporations like General Motors and organizations like the U.S. Army.

I share this here because the Internet is a legitimate business and educational channel. Like any fly-by-night money order, cash-for-gold side street vendor, some people will open their virtual doors with the intention of fleecing the public or churning cash. I suggest they will not get even as far as the cash-for-gold fleecemaster. The Internet is designed for integrity. Internet Joe needs to have valuable wares he is exchanging for income. If not, he'll be sniffed out and escorted out of town.

So if integrity is the bedrock of business, the Internet is the place where it is most solid. You wouldn't want to do business with the fleecemaster. On the Internet, you have even less chance of doing that than you do at the carnival coming through town.

For Internet Joe, this is good news. The foundational principle of all business is that the owner must have integrity to conduct business successfully and continually. Nowhere is this more likely than in the place where one star versus five stars, the comment box and the online review are available to everyone.

So, if like me, you are concerned that perhaps a virtual business might be less legitimate than a storefront on Main Street, my friend was right. It's for real, and that means you must be, too.

Besides integrity, Internet Joe has a few other characteristics that ideally suit him for success in a rapidly unfolding New Economy. Internet Joe is:

> ***Nimble***: He assembled the pieces necessary to build an online presence.
>
> ***Flexible:*** He is working his way around obstacles and making adjustments as the terrain changes daily. Software updates that change the way his online meeting service functions? He's got that.
>
> ***Responsive***: He is always on for his customers. Customers get answers from his smartphone on the road, his tablet on vacation and his home office on a 24/7 global schedule.
>
> ***Personal***: When your name is out there, your Facebook, Pinterest and far more private information is a click away.

When it comes to the New Economy, fleecemasters need not apply.

Day 11: Integrity

WITHOUT INTEGRITY, YOU can stop reading right now. Don't waste your time trying to lead an organization, or even yourself, because if you do not have integrity in all you do, you cannot perform any of the other necessary actions required to lead a successful organization.

What is integrity? Integrity is more than not cheating on your expense account. It is integrity in your treatment of all people, your communications written and oral, and the commitments that you make. If you say one thing to one person and another thing to someone else, don't expect anyone to listen to you or follow you. They cannot follow you because you have proven that you cannot be trusted; if they follow you, they don't know where they'll end up.

If there is any incongruity in your actions or words, you will lose the respect and trust of your business associates and everyone else who knows you. This applies not only to all your business dealings, but to all your dealings in life. You can't be one person in your public life and another person in your private life. Without integrity, you have nothing.

A person with integrity is one that is wholly integrated. All pieces of their life line up and make sense. A fully integrated person acts from the same core of values in all their actions, at work with their employees and coworkers, at home with their family and with their friends at the gym. Integrity is about trust and consistency.

When people let you into their world, whether it is on screen or through a product or service, you must deserve a certain basic level of trust. People with integrity are honest in all cases which is respectful of others. People who are used to treating others with respect can be expected to treat customers with respect, too. It is a behavior that comes naturally.

People with integrity have nothing to hide. What you see is the actual sum of the man or woman. This is important for several reasons. Generosity tends to accompany integrity. People who are fully integrated are free to be open and that means they are free to share their ideas, their friends, their lives and their resources. Aa a corollary to generosity, people with integrity usually have an abundance mentality. They aren't hoarders. The openness is a pre-requisite to have a giving personality, one that believes there is enough to go around. An open hand gives and receives in a virtuous cycle.

Another quality of people of integrity is their outward focus. The natural integration of their lives means that their business is a member of the community it serves. In the internet world, some entrepreneurs have a global focus so that community can be near or far.

An internet entrepreneur may be the leader of a company of one as a solopreneur or may lead a company of hundreds. But the same rules apply. As the leader of your organization, integrity is the make-or-break personal quality.

Integrity is the foundation of success in any venture and it is particularly critical to long-term successful leadership at any level, and entrepreneurship is no exception.

Day 12: Creativity

PETER DIAMANDIS, PRESIDENT of Singularity University and Founder of the XPrize, is famous for promoting "moonshot thinking," as are the people at Google X. Moonshot thinking, as Diamandis describes it, doesn't seek to achieve 10% sales growth but rather 10X more sales. Moonshot thinking is at the heart of the entrepreneurial spirit driving our culture into the New Economy. It is a creative kind of boundless that sees where nothing is and imagines what can be, full blown, in color, in 3D.

Entrepreneurs who will succeed into the next decades have a 360-degree view of the world and it is magnified by a high-powered telescope. When the world was more linear, it was enough for an entrepreneur to see around corners and make an educated guess about where the world, and his business, and the two are going together. An entrepreneur who merely sees around the next corner isn't seeing far enough to guide a business into the New Economy.

Success calls for vision and creativity that combines what we know now with what we are working on, and what we haven't yet figured out. It calls for the kind of creativity that called forth the light bulb, the airplane and David. It requires the kind of creativity usually associated with the arts, creativity that calls into being something that has no grounding in the present and can't be imagined by the minds of others because it is uniquely yours.

Creativity calls for the right brain, something we're not used to employing when making business decisions. It calls for the left brain in cooperation with the right brain. Internet Joe can make cross-brain connections. He is wired to think out of the box ("Box? What box? I didn't see any box!") and yet to organize his thoughts in a way that his imaginings are useable and replicable. Viable businesses aren't built on one-offs after all.

Because creativity pulls in so many different skills and types of intelligence, great products and services are mostly built by cooperative teams. Creativity can and should be managed to result in something truly valuable. Great project managers who understand the creative process and can coral moonshot thinking are essential members of these teams, and every entrepreneur needs a good project manager if they aren't one themselves.

Creativity isn't a lone enterprise as it might be portrayed: a baggy-eyed, frizzle-haired Einstein sleepless and obsessed. Yes, creative entrepreneurs need to be *very* creative to envision what can be. Speed is key and acceleration happens when teams multiply their vision geometrically and project managers assemble the pieces into viable products and services.

Creativity is a team sport. Dream, be agile and connected.

Day 13: Adventurous

ENTREPRENEURSHIP IS NOT for the faint of heart. Actually, leadership of any sort is not for the weak-kneed, and taking this trip into the new frontier requires stamina and hard work. Risk-taking is at the core of starting a business and putting your time, resources and reputation on the line. To move forward taking resources and reputation along for the ride certainly requires an adventurous spirit.

The key to successful business is to take calculated risks. That means both your experience and your instincts kick in when you make a decision. Like Indiana Jones when he stepped off the cliff into thin air, entrepreneurs have a sixth sense that when they take that footstep into the sky, a footbridge will appear.

Internet Joe understands the difference between adventure and foolhardiness.

He is adventurous. He is willing to spend enormous amounts of time and money (often investor money) to execute his creative vision. He is building a business and making promises to customers that he will be there to deliver on his promises. He is also promising employees that they can count on him and that it is safe to bet some of their life and livelihood participating in the vision.

Internet Joe is not foolhardy, though. He is backed by a good business plan or at least a professional grounding in what he is doing. As I mentioned the first day, Internet Joe probably landed on his own after a stint in a major corporation. He has a finely-honed sense of quality and what it takes to build his vision. The adventure is taking on the opportunity to execute it in a whole new way, serve new markets, create products and services where none existed.

If he has venture capital or a crowdsourced project, people have already vetted his credentials. The risk has a strong likelihood of an upside for investors. If he is self-funded, he needs to execute good judgment and seek the advice of close associates as he moves forward.

In either case, at the core, Internet Joe is taking some risk. Many ventures are well-vetted by professional investors, many people build businesses based on solid skills, and yet the annals of business are littered with failures within the first two years.

Success is not a guarantee and the odds are not with you, at least the first time. So, an entrepreneurial undertaking, my friends, does indeed call on a sense of adventure. Who knows where you will wind up?

Pepper your sense of adventure with calculated, educated, well-advised moves to increase your chances for success.

Day 14: Confidence

CONFIDENCE HAS TWO meanings.

In relation to business, we think about the assurance of self. Self-assurance means one believes in oneself enough to trust their own decisions. They take measured risks and can make hard decisions because self-assured people believe they have the capacity to act correctly.

The second definition of confidence is to hold something close and keep it in secret. When I tell you something in confidence, I trust that you will not broadcast it. The term "con man' in the vernacular means someone who pulls tricks on someone else. But it derives from the term "confidence man" or one who acts in secret.

Let me suggest that it requires both types of confidence to run today's entrepreneurial business in the New Economy.

First and foremost, entrepreneurs in the New Economy need the self-assurance to operate in the global environment, make assessments and act quickly. After all, the universe loves speed and the spoils go to the person able to grab opportunities as they arise. Even more accurately, the spoils go to the entrepreneur who grabs opportunities just before they arrive. He sees markets that don't yet exist or envisions ways to serve existing markets in ways that others do not see. The ability to act on unrealized markets and opportunities ahead of their manifestation requires much self-assurance.

The second definition of confidence, the ability to hold things closely and quietly, also plays an important role in entrepreneurial success. All of the advantages of the global market on the Internet everywhere, always and everything, also mean that the opportunities that are not yet realized are also evident for anyone who has eyes to see. For someone who imagines the possibilities, it is important to hold your vision close to your inside team long enough to realize it but briefly enough to bring it into full realization before someone else does.

Quick, quiet, assured. These are the behaviors of the new entrepreneur at the top of his or her game.

Day 15: Knowledge

KNOWLEDGE, CONFIDENCE AND a sense of adventure are the entrepreneurial trifecta. One or two makes someone a great employee, but a successful entrepreneur needs all three.

Imagine confidence and a sense of adventure without knowledge – you have a risk taker who has no context and who will not win the respect of employees and customers. There is a place in your startup for this person – perhaps cleaning windows on the 100th floor – but not at the helm.

What about knowledge and confidence without a sense of adventure? You have a good researcher and expert who won't step out of their comfort zone. There is a place in your organization for this person in the lab, but not at the helm.

Now imagine knowledge and a sense of adventure without confidence – you have a risk taker who will step out but is unable to follow through. There is a place for this person in your startup, perhaps as the pitch person, but not at the helm.

An entrepreneur in the New Economy enters the global marketplace with a certain set of knowledge and skills to support their confidence and sense of adventure. That trifecta is the ticket to enter in the global entrepreneurial sweepstakes.

A successful entrepreneur in the New Economy has a learning mindset because the environment is always in motion. Remember our discussion earlier about the pace of knowledge and the rapid acquisition of data: half of what we know was not available yesterday!

What Internet Joe knows may have been true yesterday. However, with the rapid expanse of knowledge and data collection, that truth may be different today. In fact, if you are starting a new business, there is a pretty good chance you can assume you are operating with outdated information even as you develop your products and services.

In a fully interconnected, 24/7 marketplace, knowledge isn't static. It's fluid. A business in the New Economy is a learning organization and that requires a learning CEO. The leader sets the example. There is an old saying that "leaders are readers". More accurately, leaders are learners. As situations materialize and unfold, leaders can process what is happening, adjust their product, service or approach based on constantly changing data.

The world is always in beta, and successful entrepreneurs practice agility. Think permanent beta and constant learning, and you have the essence of knowledge in the New Economy.

Week 3
Internet Infrastructure

Day 16: Imagine Leadership and Management

THE TRADITIONAL ORGANIZATIONAL chart is a construct left over from Alfred Sloan's leadership at General Motors in the early 20th Century. That, my friends, is 100 years ago.

In the 1980s, the hierarchical organization chart was challenged by enterprises that found products were better built when workers had ownership of their production. The philosophy of pushing decision making down to the employee flattened the organizational chart somewhat and, as a result, relationships became "matrixed" – people had multiple layers of reporting and responsibility, and accountability was spread throughout the organization.

The shift away from top-down thinking has been gradual. It paved the way for entrepreneurs in the New Economy to be comfortable spreading responsibility, accountability and rewards across the organization based on performance, not based on role.

Leadership and management in the New Economy is about vision and goalsetting. It is about being able to get out in front of the parade with a baton while respecting the fact that without a parade, Internet Joe is leading no one.

And here is where the distinction between leadership and management takes a leap.

True leadership isn't conferred as much as it is earned. True leaders are people who others follow, in fact emulate, for their innate qualities. This harkens back to our first and most important quality of leadership, and that is integrity. People naturally follow someone they trust; they know they will wind up somewhere worth going. That requires a bit of a track record.

Management skills can be learned. Management is about the ability to align and assign resources to achieve goals. Managers don't require the kinds of rigorous traits of a true leader, but they do require consistency, persistence and organizational skills. Managers don't need to be leaders.

But great leaders get nowhere without great management of resources. If an entrepreneur is not a great organizer, it is critical that they hire one. A great idea, even with enthusiastic followers, goes nowhere without someone to arrange the resources in straight lines all headed in the same direction.

Leadership and management don't have to be embodied in the same individual. They do, however, need to be together at all times for efficient allocation of resources. An entrepreneur in the New Economy needs efficient organizational alignment with wise distribution of responsibilities and accountability even though your business map will not resemble, even remotely, Alfred Sloan's hierarchical organizational chart at GM.

A successful entrepreneur today is not at the top of their organization. They are in the lead, and that is a very different position.

Day 17: Imagine Finance

FINANCING IN THE New Economy has two radical differentiators from the old days. One is the way in which you attract investors, and the second is how much it actually costs to start up your Internet business.

Let's talk about direct access to investors.

Remember the good old days, say the first decade of the 21st Century, when a prospective entrepreneur seeking funding would schlep their slide deck into a startup incubator and present to the veteran investor gatekeepers who doled out wisdom about business plans, management teams and boards of directors?

Gone? Not quite. But is that model still the most viable avenue for startup funding? Not even!

With crowdsourcing and crowdfunding ideas like Kickstarter, you can find your idea by throwing it out to the Internet and letting the investors come to you. You can raise a little money taking donations and small sums from interested Internet friends and advocates with a "Donate Here" button. Or you can raise serious millions using more structured funding mechanisms that require investors meet certain criteria.

For an entrepreneur in the New Economy, this simply means that Internet Joe can bypass more traditional and restrictive funding mechanisms and go straight to the public.

Startup investment can be minimal.

As an entrepreneur in the New Economy, Internet Joe has nearly limitless and cheap/free resources at his fingertips – those same fingertips tapping on the keyboard. You can start up a business idea with minimal capital. And you can get world-class advice for the price of an Internet connection.

There are brilliant people sharing their startup knowledge for nothin'. The saying "you get what you pay for" does not apply in this case. This rich vein of Internet resources in the exception that proves the rule. In fact, the incredible free startup advice and business acumen, market research and tools to reach a global market cost close to no money at all.

In his great program Product Launch Formula, Jeff Walker shares the secret that you can actually sell products that you haven't yet developed. It's not a scam. It's about meeting your customers where their need exists.

You sell the product then produce it in response to buyers. The only catch, the big asterisk, is that you had better know what you are doing so you can deliver when the time comes. If you are selling lamps, you'd better be able to produce them when the orders come rolling in. The idea is not sleazy. Nope. It's actually excellent business advice that has been around for decades: Develop your prototypes and first-generation iterations of products and services in cooperation with your customers. By designing products as you sell them, you are developing products the marketplace actually wants and needs.

Transactions in the New Economy are global, virtual and have no boundaries.

One of my favorite New Economy gurus is Ray Kurzweil, the innovative genius who wrote the seminal work regarding all things future, *The Singularity is Near*. In his 2005 epic work, he straightened out my main misconception about the global economy. Until I read his book, I was stuck in the idea that all money and value is tied to concrete productivity. I was just plain wrong. Having projected the Internet of all things before we ever heard of IoT, Kurzweil perceived that the value of the Internet changed the definition of value. Money has changed because it is now a fluid concept based on the nearly limitless possibilities of the global computer mind which creates exponential relationships that expand past our individual ability to make connections. Given that premise, he predicted that the Dow Jones Industrial Average would triple in ten years. In 2005, the DJIA stood at a the then-unprecedented 10,000 and to some seemed wildly over-valued then. The idea that the stock market would triple was ludicrous. The in 2008, the global economy crashed and bubbles like the real estate market also burst. Also, the dry bulk index hit an all-town low, indicating that global shipping crashed. What did the DJIA do in response? It continued to rise.

Traditionalists continued to scratch their heads. But futurists just sat back and watched because they know that the measure of value has changed and the DJIA reflects latent value as the economy rearranges itself. In 2015, the DJIA stood at 18,000 and traditional watchers shook their heads saying it continues to be overvalued.

It tripled in 15 years. Close enough.

For those who are stuck in the world of the dry bulk index and the movement of tangibles in the market, the stock market ascent appears to be smoke and mirrors. When I read Kurzweil I understood, finally, that my attachments to things like physical products and national monetary systems were outdated.

Finance in the New Economy is global and virtual, but it doesn't mean it isn't real. Quite the opposite. The inherent value in the instantaneous transmission of knowledge and the ability to transact with anyone, anywhere, anytime has reinvented the basis of the financial system.

As Internet Joe builds his business on this very solid foundation of the virtual New Economy, he is plugging into nearly limitless abundance.

The new rules of finance have yet to be written. Entrepreneurs are writing them as they build the New Economy.

Day 18: Imagine Marketing

ONE OF THE great advances of the 20th Century was the development of the field of marketing. As industrialists were able to mass produce clothing, cars, homes and candy bars, they needed to promote those things to a public who many not have known they needed them.

Psychology and sociology combined with imperatives to maximize business profitability and the science of markets was born. Where markets existed, they were exploited. Where markets did not exist, they were created.

You know you need a home, but you didn't know you need a certain type of kitchen appliance or configuration of closets until marketers told you. You know you need a car to get to work, but marketers let you know which badge need to be attached to the hood to display power, status and sex appeal.

Marketing attaches meaning to the products and services we consume. Marketing raises necessities to luxuries for a price. Marketing creates desire for products and services you didn't know you needed or wanted until subliminal desires are attached to them.

By the mid-20th Century, mass production meant that businesses could create enough products to satisfy the desires of mass markets. Mass communication through a limited number of channels using television, terrestrial radio and magazines standardized desire for mass produced products.

The Internet changed the whole world of marketing. The Internet is a personal communication device. What comes through my computer is as different from what comes through yours, as we are different from each other. No two computers deliver the same content because the content is a reflection of the fingerprint of the user. One user accesses religious content, another pornography, yet a third spends most of their time surfing the net for the best price on handbags and shoes.

How do you market to the individual on their personal communication device? Like finance, we're rewriting the discipline of marketing while we're practicing business in the New Economy.

As an Internet entrepreneur, you find your markets by searching for people who are interested in buying what you are selling. You contact them through social media using list serves, groups, blogs and following where each thread leads. When you pull on a thread, it will lead to a tapestry of related interest groups. As a business person, you know that at the end of each thread is a potential customer.

The hardest job of Internet Joe is to refine his product or service to meet the needs of a specifically defined market within the potential of a global customer base. Expect that it could take time to refine your approach. You will go through several iterations before you hit on exactly what flavor of what you offer appeals to which individuals.

In the New Economy, your customers are in New Zealand and Newfoundland. Now find them.

Day 19: Imagine Sales

ORGANIZATIONS FREQUENTLY COUPLE sales with marketing, and we'll do that here, too. When you've defined your markets, you have the basis of a sales program. As we mentioned yesterday in Imagine Marketing, your customers are connected to you by a personal communication device that delivers content that is highly individualized. Your sales strategy needs to be the same.

For example, if you are selling a weight loss system, you aren't reaching a single imagined customer about their weight with standardized sales materials. You are reaching an individual with personalized content. You can deliver emails customized with the name of prospects by leveraging the power of email lists. You can individualize your approach using your website with a "click here for patients", "click here for physicians", "click here for caregivers" approach to sales. As your potential customers "click here", they can further individualize their search for your products and services by drilling down into your website.

It is possible to individualize your approach to customers for a very low cost per touch using email and websites. You aren't just selling a special formulation to lose weight, you are sharing information that is creating a personal relationship with your customer. You can jump on a video and talk to them face-to-face. Your style, clothing, language, age and style speaks to individuals like you. You can speak directly to your personal market.

As we discussed earlier, this is where Internet Joe holds an advantage over large corporations as an entrepreneur. By leveraging social media platforms such as Twitter, Facebook, Pinterest and Instagram, your product automatically has viral potential. Internet Joe makes personal connections with people around the globe and they are all potential customers. With a few power users among your followers, you can get exposure to 250,000 people through one connection which very quickly expands to millions. On a planet with already 4.5 billion Internet-connected individuals, you have tapped into only a small fraction of potential customers and already have exceeded a 20th Century salesperson's wildest fantasies.

Bricks and mortar have been uber-ized.

Even if your business is based on live customer interactions, such as a restaurant or a hair salon, your bricks and mortar business needs an Internet presence to exist. If someone visits your town and looks for pizza, they will search for restaurants online and your business needs to be there. As a plumber, you may not think you are an Internet Joe, but online presence still makes the difference between survival and massive opportunity.

Think of the Uber business model. For drivers and homeowners plugged into the system, Uber and AirBnB provide income previously only possible with the reach of the local realtor or the "looking for a ride to California" message boards of old.

Sellers can be anybody with an Internet connection, but Internet Joe is a true entrepreneurial businessman leveraging the power of the Internet to grow sales opportunities with the immense power of global markets.

Day 20: Imagine Manufacturing

THE FLEXIBILITY OF the global markets – everywhere, everyone, all the time – means products and services be delivered from your place of business on the Internet to the customer's location in the same way. With virtual products like software, books and music, it's a natural medium. 3D printing allows some products to be assembled on site by downloading software as a blueprint to build products by the customer. Customers only need the material to create the products on location.

One of the issues with matching mass production to local markets has been transportation and warehousing of raw materials and finished products. 3D production eliminates one of these transfers.

Historically, efficient production required factories be located near the source of raw materials which could be halfway around the globe from your customers. With global markets, raw material processing happens near the source of materials which are then delivered to where final products are produced at the customer site.

Throughout history, efficiencies have grown markets. This development is no different.

While assembling products on site requires the transfer of only raw materials to the customer location, the expansion of markets grows the number of end users. Economic development happens more rapidly in areas that now need mainly an Internet connection and a reliable source of power to become a viable market for your products – both virtual and physical products.

The limiting factors remain the availability of power and water. The new entrepreneurs believe those problems can be solved, and they are actively seeking answers. As I mentioned earlier, we are very early in the New Economy and are still building the infrastructure so much of the opportunity is building the virtual roads and rails into the future.

Even in situations where finished products are mass produced in a single location and need to be transported to customers around the globe, robotics simplifies production. It reduces the number of individuals who need to be trained to assemble products to the number it takes to program and calibrate equipment. Local education and workforce availability is not a major factor in locating a factory today.

You can overcome worker fear with optimism.

Since line-driven powered machinery was invented, workers have revolted against automation fearing for their jobs. However, in each instance, peoples' lives have improved. More products are available to more people at a higher quality, and more peoples' time is freed for higher level pursuits. The promise of manufacturing in the New Economy turns on how you view progress. You can have one of two views of the world:

> View 1: You believe advances solve problems, make solutions available to more people, and raise all of humanity in waves.

> View 2: You believe knowledge is finite, all that can be known is already known, and we can't solve our problems because our known resources do not meet everyone's needs.

Entrepreneurs in the New Economy hold View 1. What lies beyond the known frontier is the place where advances for humanity lie. Internet Joe senses what exists in the unknown and moves toward it.

Day 21: Imagine Inventory and Delivery

IN TANDEM WITH global manufacturing, let's consider how to store and move physical products in the New Economy. Since time immemorial, if you live where grasses are plentiful, you lived in grass huts. People have always adapted to local resources and in the New Economy, efficient and successful communities will rely on this same strategy – but with a difference.

As we discussed yesterday when we imagined manufacturing, many products will be able to be assembled closer to their markets because 3D printing of finished products and parts will make that possible. Also, robotic manufacturing makes it possible to locate production facilities in places without consideration of the availability of many prepared workers.

Local sourcing of raw materials will re-emerge as a critical aspect of the New Economy.

Our knowledge grows about our environment every day, and we find more uses for things around us. Materials can be manufactured using chemical and biological processes. During the period of 20th Century industrialization, synthetic materials were developed. For example, clothing manufacturers didn't necessarily need wool or cotton to make clothing because they had synthetic materials. The same thing is happening with biological substances such as food and medicines which are moving from chemically-based to biologically-based.

Knowledge in the new frontier will find ways to transform available local resources into the necessary materials which should reduce the demand to transport and store raw materials.

The more we learn about chemistry and biology, the more possibilities we have to use the basic structures that compose a pineapple, for example, into materials to manufacture other products needed locally.

This will affect energy and transportation.

When requirements to transport people and materials are reduced, this necessarily results in less requisite shipping vessels and fuel. In this scenario, energy needs to be produced and consumed locally to support local raw material development and product manufacture. This lends itself to utilization of less portable and more available sources of fuel like solar and wind.

Internet Joe is thinking about the future, and the future does not resemble the present. That means a lot of limiting factors in the present, such as finite, non-renewable, transportable fuel, are not part of fueling the New Economy.

Day 22: Imagine Your Learning Organization

THE RAPID ACQUISITION and deployment of knowledge means that all organizations that plan to survive also have a process for knowledge acquisition, retention, management and transfer in their business plan. Forward thinking organizations today consider themselves learning organizations.

As an entrepreneur in the New Economy, even though you may be small, your responsibility is to not only know what is going on in your own business but contribute to the growing body of collective knowledge. Remember, all the Internet Joes around the globe are learning and building this ship together so sharing what you've learned and what you are developing is part of that responsibility and your value as a member of the global business community.

There are two parts to this knowledge acquisition and sharing. One is the internal knowledge of your individual product or service, and the second part is the external learning about the infrastructure you are building either deliberately or inadvertently by participating in the New Economy.

Your internal knowledge is important to the collective.

Whether you are operating alone, with a handful of close team members or a cast of 100s, you need to store and transfer knowledge about product development, marketing, deployment and all other aspects of your business to assure continuity. When you've built a global community of customers, they will have questions and need support. Codify, iterate, revise, update, repeat. Consider yourself in a constant state of beta.

Remember, we said that one of the advantages of Internet Joe is the ability to be agile and nimble. This requires a state of continuous learning which is a mindset of quality improvement. Because you aren't taking a large organization with you, when you learn something new, as an Internet entrepreneur you are able to capitalize on that information and pivot instantaneously.

Your external knowledge helps others, too.

The intimate relationship you develop with your customers through their personal communication devices is the basis of your ongoing learning. You are learning what works, what they like about your product and service, what needs improvement and when you haven't hit the mark.

Your systems and connections are creating the need for the kind of infrastructure required to build the New Economy. When you share what you need and what you've learned about commerce with others in the online business community, the network grows.

What we know changes every minute and what you do with it will be different than what someone else does with it. Record it. Share it. It forms the next step on the ladder raising all players.

Week 4
Your Resources

Day 23: Financing

WE HAVE ALREADY explored the potential of the effect of the changing financial realities of the New Economy on your Internet business. Some of the old gatekeepers of investment capital have been supplanted by the ability to reach out directly to potential investors.

For small entrepreneurs, you may only need a few thousand dollars and some grit. With the amount of free and low-cost resources at your disposal, you can start a substantial business with a little startup cash and some imagination. That means many people can build their business out of pocket.

There are many benefits to funding your own enterprise. You have no debt except to yourself. You retain control of the business and you own it 100% outright. And you can spend your time on your business, not courting potential investors. If you can do it, self-financing is the way to go.

If you need to attract investors for a larger idea, you can go directly to individuals. Wise investors (which are the type you want) will vet you and help you by making sure your idea is viable and you are able to execute it professionally. Consider wise investors another advantage that you take into your venture.

You may be the person who imagines the concept, but you don't want to go it alone. Wise investors will look at the credentials of your support system as well as your own ability to execute your ideas. The more advisors and team members you have in your corner, even those part-timers and professional friends are very important to your success. You want others to help you hone your ideas, promote your products and services, and be your cheerleaders on days when you need one.

When you are looking to attract capital, that team will make or break your ability to do so.

Be strategic about your partnerships. Build bench strength where you have weaknesses. Make sure the human resources you have onboard support your mission and can conduct all the internal business processes required to operate legally, ethically and with solid financial plans.

Finally, be realistic about the amount of financing that you need. If you overestimate, you will spend your time raising money for things you don't need or could easily and more quickly do for yourself. If you underestimate, you will get only partway to goal. A realistic plan is to start your business in small and manageable chunks with the resources and financing at your disposal, and when the marketplace responds with interest and orders, you can raise the stakes.

Day 24: Revenue

AT THE OUTSET, most people will start their business with investor or personal financing. In short order, a viable business in the New Economy will generate revenue. Revenue generation is the money you bring in from customers for your products and services. While you won't necessarily run your business from customer revenue from Day One, you should be able to do so within a few months.

With a global online business, you need to find a way to validate payment in a form that is recognized on both sides of the transaction. Because your business is global and virtual, your revenue will ideally be global and virtual, too. The issue of valid payment for revenue generation is part of building the infrastructure for the New Economy. This issue begat payment forms like bitcoin, also known generically in its many forms as cryptocurrency.

Ultimately, the New Economy will form the basis for a global currency simply because it makes sense. When global business was conducted only among large corporations or a limited number of globe-trotting individuals, currency exchange was somewhat cumbersome but manageable. In a commerce system where individuals are trading among each other constantly, a common global currency makes sense.

Global currency is one of the hot potatoes that causes governments and political interests enormous discomfort for reasons that go beyond our scope here. But let me suggest that, just as commerce led the way to break down barriers among different people as merchants set sail for spices in India and silk in China, global Internet commerce will trump parochial interests as the new entrepreneur needs to find a verifiable way to receive payment from customers.

Global pricing is a tangential issue to global payment. Pricing is often locally controlled and regulated, especially in certain industries. Products and services on the Internet eventually will create an environment where value is rationalized across economies as the world merges into one seamless trade opportunity.

Global trade does not have to be a hot potato, either. But for reasons that are beyond our discussion here, the opportunity to expand commerce and increase opportunities for human beings everywhere will eventually de-fuse those issues. A global currency doesn't have to be a painful dislocation, but rather it can occur as a slow, organic and natural progression of the growth of human knowledge and potential. Forays into bitcoin and similar ideas demonstrate the process.

As we discussed earlier, war is historically the way that humans expanded their influence. The emergence of a global merchant class slowly but constantly changed the tools of influence expansion from blunt-edged brute force power to soft economic power expanding among individuals. The individual entrepreneur with access to global markets and interconnected billions of people will complete this transition.

The need for a medium of global exchange among individuals trading on global basis will have effects far beyond the practical solution of making value connections using a common currency. Remember the Arab Spring in Syria referenced earlier? It was a movement of humans connected with humans who connected the dots. With the incentive of global markets for individual entrepreneurs, expect the global currency further breaking down barriers among humans.

Day 25: Human Capital

I HAVE HEARD some people say that they don't like the term "human capital" because it sounds cold and impersonal. Actually, when I first heard it years ago, I liked it for exactly the opposite reason. Human "capital" describes the value of workers to an enterprise. Whereas labor is typically counted as a cost, capital describes it as an asset. Without knowledge workers in the New Economy, a business has no valuable assets.

Last week, we discussed the importance of enterprises as learning organizations since knowledge and information are growing exponentially by the minute. In a knowledge-based economy, humans are the most important resource.

The knowledge-based worker turns the idea that machines displace workers on its head. Workers who tend to machines or build widgets that can be assembled by robots are underutilized. One study by the Martin School at Oxford predicts that 48% of American jobs alone will be lost to robotics in the next 20 years. This is good news, because as the New Economy grows, workers grow in importance and stature. Rather than being displaced by machines, knowledge workers are freed for higher level tasks, tasks that use more of their innate abilities and engage their interests. Higher level tasks in a knowledge economy move workers closer to full actualization of their potential.

A 2015 Gallup Poll found that 70% of American hate their jobs. I am going to guess that statistic can be pretty closely correlated anywhere on the planet. Being freed from loathsome employment is the job of Internet Joe and the people on his team. As the lowest, ugliest jobs disappear, the entrepreneur and his creative staff can enjoy serving a growing, global, online market of potential customers who will consume vast amounts of innovative human resources. Workers' displacement by machines has always resulted in rising the living standard of all despite fears of laborers during the period of dislocation. The accelerated process in a rapidly-expanding knowledge economy should be no different.

So, "human capital" it is.

As you prepare to hire knowledge workers in the New Economy, consider these things.

Internet Joe is building his online empire on the shoulders of knowledge workers. Deep knowledge workers. Highly specialized people who may be in his employ or may be supplying services as a vendor.

The human capital resources needed by the entrepreneur in the New Economy are the best available in the world, literally in the world, serving the world. Knowledge workers as human capital are always learning, because growth is joy.

As an entrepreneur, you will be supporting workers who find fulfillment in what they do. That kind of leadership will require a different brand of guidance than leadership in the past that was focused on motivating workers to perform repetitive or onerous tasks. Entrepreneurial leadership in the New Economy is more about clarifying the vision than motivating your employees.

Knowledge workers on your team will sometimes lead you, and that is a perfectly acceptable turn of events when you are working with highly valuable human capital.

Day 26: Buildings and Machinery

AFTER YESTERDAY'S DISCUSSION of human capital, it is on to a discussion of the more traditional role of capital as assets in the form of buildings and machinery.

The large office complex will not disappear, but a lot of new entrepreneurs will find they can start at home or need a lot less real space for an online business.

Successful businesses will always need an official location. While Internet Joe maybe able to start in a home-based office, growth makes an official office site important. If a business is largely virtual and run by a team that is scattered in offices throughout the world, home offices may suffice as ground zero.

Even small entrepreneurs would do well to consider temporary or flex office space for an official address and, more importantly, to take the business up a notch.

When a young entrepreneur has assembled a team around him or her, it is best to co-locate everyone to gain the benefit of team thinking and create brainstorming. So, even office-based online small businesses gain value from official office space.

Businesses will grow beyond the initial stages of the small, online entrepreneur.

Your small business may require more than a few desks, computers and routers. Your idea may require lab space or assembly and warehouse space. At some point in your growth, expect that warehouse, transport and meeting space may be required. Plan for growth in your financial projections, and that includes physical, commercial space.

Customers of global businesses in the New Economy still expect to see an address with a GPS location. A location grounds you and makes you more real for your virtual customers. Buildings and machinery are still part of a business in the New Economy. They just don't take center stage as they once did. In the Old Economy, the first thing you might do when you open a business is to lease office or retail space; in the New Economy, it may be the last thing that you do.

Buildings and machinery are smaller, more flexible, leased and temporary. Remember that as an entrepreneur in the New Economy, you are always ready to pivot.

Whatever it is, if you can do it here, you can usually do it there, too. The difference is that your physical presence gives weight to your enterprise but won't weigh it down.

Day 27: Communications Network

THE COMMUNICATIONS NETWORK is at the heart of the business model in the New Economy. A communications plan with your team and your customers is no longer a "nice to have", it is absolutely essential to your survival.

It doesn't matter whether your products are virtual or physical, you need a full-time communications network in place to keep your business viable.

Your communications network is based on your Internet provider, but it only starts there. Communications includes both the platform for communicating, the software that you use and the web of relationships that you have.

Beyond a reliable Internet connection, you need to be running software that is compatible with everyone else. Most of the web-based communications platforms run for everyone just about everywhere and are easy to use. Your communications platforms need to be universal because your relationships with customers and team members rely on their functioning.

You start with a reliable email service. You add a service that allows you to deliver large files such as Dropbox or another file transfer protocol provider. You add a team-friendly platform where you can gather everyone for a face-to-face virtual meeting such as Skype. Then you can layer any number of software programs that enhance your experience.

You'll need messaging services. Email services. Social platforms.

Even if you are technically savvy, expect to have a technical support person or three at your disposal. If you have someone whose job it is to manage the technical communications issues upon which your

Internet business relies, it frees you to concentrate on the pieces that you can't replicate, which is all the value that your specialty brings to the marketplace.

I am always impressed and amazed at the stories of entrepreneurs who dedicated nights, weekends and months to mastering communications platforms to build their businesses. But, at some point, sooner rather than later as revenue arrives, it is a good idea to liberate yourself from maintaining the networks upon which your business depends and put that into professional hands.

Your ability to communicate with your customers and your staff is the lifeblood of your business in the New Economy, and it shouldn't be jeopardized to save a few dollars or because you think that you can do it well enough. Well enough isn't good enough as you become a bigger player, even a marginally bigger player.

Put your money into your communications platform as one of your first investments. It is the one that will keep you alive.

Day 28: Education and Training

OVER THE LAST few weeks, we discussed the knowledge worker, the learning organization and human capital. All these concepts are built on this one essential tool, which is the basic education and formalized training of yourself and your team.

Real value begins with a solid foundational learning that begins almost at birth because there is so much to know, and we know so much more about how we learn. Real physical school beyond mother, father and caregivers usually begins in preschool and is enhanced by formal elementary education of young children. By the time young teens enter higher education, their paths are often clear.

In the U.S., as children grow into the teen years, the opportunities begin to splinter into specializations in the form of publicly-funded magnet and alternative schools, and for those who can afford it, private schools where education is usually more competitive and tracked toward certain university programs.

Some foundational learning can be had online but most still exists almost entirely in a physical setting or classroom building. However, university learning is moving more online, which means that both the entrepreneur and his or her team may have specialized learning from a global, online university. Private, for-profit online universities often do not have the rigorous entry requirements of a physical university, but the coursework is comparable.

Ongoing adult learning is facilitated through the workplace, often supported by the workplace or self-driven, using free or very inexpensive, non-degreed materials available through organizations online.

Nothing speaks more loudly about the way humans seek fulfillment and self-actualization than the proliferation of for-profit online universities, professionally sponsored educational forums and classes, and private businesses dedicated to providing educational products for personal and professional development.

In a knowledge-based economy, workers are lifelong learners, As the entrepreneur, you will be a lifelong learner absorbing massive amounts of information coming at you. Some of your education will be used to just give yourself and your organization the ability to sort and curate information coming at you so that you can home in on the relevant information to drive your own business forward.

Take advantage of being an educated consumer of lifelong learning so you can intelligently filter the onslaught of information you need to absorb to operate effectively in the New Economy.

Day 29: Health and Wellness

AS AN ENTREPRENEUR, you are responsible for your own, and possibly your team's, health and wellness. A study released in June 2015 found that almost one-third of workers would quit their jobs if they did not have access to healthcare benefits through their employers. Health, wellness and employment are related.

Not only are employees concerned about healthcare benefits while in your employ, a smart business owner is concerned about the health and wellness of his or her employees in the New Economy. After all, wellness is correlated to both physical and mental health, and those things have a bearing on productivity. A healthy worker is a contented and productive worker.

Knowledge workers are engaged in activities that fulfill them personally. They are not disconnected from their work as the manufacturing line workers of the industrial era. You and your team will operate at peak efficiency when the mind-body-spirit connection is acknowledged and encouraged.

Health and wellness is more than providing a health plan. For you and anyone on your team, health is about fitness, eating well, and having a positive mental attitude. All those things that contribute to holistic health affect the performance of your business.

You can put your enterprise on more solid footing by making sure you are taking good care of yourself, and that you are making health and wellness opportunities available to members of your team. Beyond funding doctor and hospital insurance, employee health and wellness can be supported by online and telemedicne services that monitor function, give feedback to exercise and diet efforts and support people during difficult personal times.

Smart entrepreneurs are sensitive to the mind, body and spirit connection for themselves and those around them.

Day 30: Entrepreneur's Checklist

ENTREPRENEURS, IT IS time to move.

Do you know the next 5 steps you need to take *now*?

Over the last 30days, we've discussed the ways in which yesterday is over, and today's markets are not the same as they'll be tomorrow. You need to be ready to pivot. You must continually assess and re-position as conditions change. Success loves speed. That is because the New Economy is knowledge-based, nimble, and driven by technology – with the Internet as its infrastructure. Old rules don't apply.

If you are an entrepreneur in this environment, working alone is not a way to navigate this wild frontier. You need to plan for the unique challenges and issues you will face in all facets of your business – marketing & competitive analysis, sales, finances, vendors & sourcing, labor & management, training & employee development – not to mention how to balance your business drive with your personal life to achieve maximum performance.

If you are just beginning or partway down the path already, make sure you:

1. Define realistic objectives – write down your vision
2. Create hands-on strategic plans – have 90-day plans and a one-year plan
3. Employ winning entrepreneurship tactics – master the art of permanent beta
4. Work with all your critical stakeholders – customers, employees, vendor and investors
5. Motivate employees to share your enthusiasm – share your vision and create team goals

Afterword: A Post-COVID-19, Non-Fragile World

Steward your business with both the local and global connections at your disposal, using all the technology available to advance your idea, and you can play a major role in the New Economy.

LANGUAGE LEADS THE way. If you want to put your finger in the wind of public sentiment or policy, listen to the words people use. In business circles, the word "resilience" has been replaced by the word "non-fragile". That subtle difference speaks volumes about how we see ourselves, and it presages the kind of hard times that we *think* are ahead.

"Resilience" speaks of inherent strength – strength of character, depth of resources, and the ability to adapt. "Non-fragility" emphasizes weakness, and we are reminded of the fragile nature of life itself. Is our transportation system fragile? Are our supply chains weak? Is our food supply unsustainable?

We want to emphasize our resilience and our potential.

Actually, our future is the one that we imagine it to be. Because as a man thinketh portends our reality. That is not to deny the reality that our world – in the face of one microscopic pathogen - was shown to be a naked man, skittering across the stage holding a blanket across his torso. But we have the ability to think, and from those thoughts, we can act our way toward a world that embraces all the good that is possible and rejects resurrecting the things that had outlived their usefulness and, in some cases, had turned rotten as they've aged.

We are headed toward the future on hyperdrive.

The Dow Jones Industrial Average (DJIA) refuses to tank even amidst historic unemployment. Some skeptics attribute that solely to the Federal Reserve Bank of the U.S. pumping unprecedented amounts of liquidity (U.S. dollars) into the system. Because the stock markets can sometimes lead sentiment, rather than follow it, let me suggest that there is an underlying bullishness about the economy because it is shifting into a new reality more aligned with the kind of possibilities outlined in this little book. I am suggesting that the stock market is discounting the present because it sees the future. And the economic readjustment period has just encountered warp speed due to a pandemic that shut down the old way of doing things. When we ramp up again, we ramp up into the future having just imploded the old system.

For those who follow such things, we knew the old system was imploding. Our global relationships relative to the supply chain (think China) were already changing with an increased emphasis on national independence and more closely politically aligned partnerships. The Federal Reserve had already started pumping massive amounts of liquidity into the U.S. banking system 4 months before the pandemic even had a name. When oil's price per barrel of crude went into negative territory on April 21, 2020 to minus $40 a barrel, it was not just in response to the pandemic. Our global supply chain and trade had already started to slow for other reasons. If oil went negative, perhaps we need to go positive because that indicator presages change. It means many of the changes discussed in this book are underway.

In the New Economy, we are encouraged to make a few new moves, just like the old moves, but better.

Here are a few directions to consider as we feel our way forward in the dark.

First, all politics and relationships are local and person-to-person.

That also applies to business. Nurture personal relationships and imagine ways your business can flourish in your local geography, no matter what you do. We have discovered how fragile our supply chains can be, how quickly transportation and production can stop. We discovered in a harsh way the importance of local business to meet physical and psychological needs. You can play a role in keeping things moving by making sure you are sustainable locally. Be part of the Main Street movement.

Also, consider the converse.

The power of the internet anchors the New Economy. No matter how local your business and relationships, nurture your global connections. When you stay connected to all the best ideas and people available to you in the global economy, you will continue to improve your own prospects in your backyard.

Let's wrap up and return to Day 1.

New ideas spread through wars, conquest and trade. The pandemic may give us the opportunity to bypass the war and go straight to the reward of moving the world ahead through an economic revolution aided by technology. After all, aren't all revolutions economic at their inception?

Ask the British subjects living in North America about their opposition to "taxation without representation". Or the French common man about his servitude to King Louis XVI (that one ended badly in a dictatorship – take heed!). Or the Southern U.S. plantation owners when the north threatened their economic model built on slavery. Human history is built upon populations pushing back against entrenched power and failing systems.

The pandemic is an opportunity to recalibrate the economic system, enjoy a flattening of power and financial wealth, and truly liberate individuals to embrace their personal power and express the full measure of their productivity.

Or not.

We choose.

www.ingramcontent.com/pod-product-compliance
Lightning Source LLC
Chambersburg PA
CBHW020455220526
45464CB00002B/1002